Bombing the Thinker Darren C. Demaree

A pioneering publishing house dedicated to creating intelligent, vivid books. Established to inform, educate, entertain and provoke.

A Backlash Press Book
First published 2018

www.backlashpress.com

SCB Distributors
15608 South New Century Drive
Gardena, CA 90248, USA

Book designer: The Scrutineer, Rachael Adams.

Printed and bound by Ingram.

ISBN: 978-0-9955999-6-3

All rights reserved. No part of this publication may be reproduced, stored in a retrieval system or transmitted in any form or by any means, electronic, mechanical, photocopying, recording or otherwise, without permission of the copyright holder.

Copyright © Darren C. Demaree
The moral rights of the author have been asserted.

Bombing the Thinker

Darren C. Demaree

Bombing the Thinker Darren C. Demaree

Contents

A LETTER TO AUGUSTE RODIN ABOUT USELESS WINE	/ 9
1970	/ 11
A UNIQUE AND HAUNTING BEAUTY	/ 13
A DAMAGED THINKER #2	/ 15
A DAMAGED THINKER #3	/ 17
ALMOST THE POINT OF ART	/ 19
AN ACCEPTANCE OF ART	/ 21
BLOWN UP BY RADICAL PROTESTORS	/ 23
IT WAS IMPERATIVE TO REMOVE THE OIL	/ 25
A DAMAGED THINKER #12	/ 27
A DAMAGED THINKER #13	/ 29
A LETTER TO AUGUSTE RODIN, ASKING ABOUT HIS OTHER CASTS OF THE THINKER	/ 31
NOT CROP, NOT HUSK	/ 33
AN EYE-CATCHING MEMORIAL OF MINDLESS VIOLENCE	/ 35
A LETTER TO AUGUSTE RODIN, EXPLAINING THE BOMBING OF THE THINKER	/ 37
"DAMAGED 24TH OF MARCH 1970" WRITTEN IN SMALLER LETTERS	/ 39
THE RADICAL WEATHERMAN	/ 41
A DAMAGED THINKER #16	/ 43
A DAMAGED THINKER #18	/ 45
A DAMAGED THINKER #20	/ 47
A DAMAGED THINKER #24	/ 49
NO ONE WAS EVER ARRESTED	/ 51
A LETTER TO AUGUSTE RODIN, ASKING ABOUT HIS OTHER CASTS OF THE THINKER	/ 53
FREE FROM ARREST	/ 55
A COLD AND LONELY PIECE OF ART	/ 57
DEEP PITS	/ 59
FINISHING A SHERMAN LEE QUOTE	/ 61
A DAMAGED THINKER #29	/ 63
ORIGINALLY NAMED THE POET	/ 65
STABALIZED, WASHED, AND WAXED	/ 67
THE MONUMENT NOW REFLECTS THE ACTS OF INSANE MEN	/ 69

Bombing the Thinker Darren C. Demaree

A DAMAGED THINKER #34	/ 71
A DAMAGED THINKER #36	/ 73
A DAMAGED THINKER #38	/ 75
A DAMAGED THINKER #40	/ 77
"THE LAST OPTION OF MOUNTING THE SCULPTURE IN ITS DAMAGED STATE ALSO HAD SIGNIFICANT ETHICAL IMPLICATIONS"	/ 79
THERE WAS STILL A PEDESTAL	/ 81
WHERE THE HEAD AND SHOULDER HIT THE PAVEMENT	/ 83
INCRALAC COATING	/ 85
A DAMAGED THINKER #47	/ 87
A DAMAGED THINKER #48	/ 89
ALMOST FREE	/ 91
CHASING THE LOGIC OF A BOMBING	/ 93
AN AVOIDANCE OF ART	/ 95
A LETTER TO AUGUSTE RODIN ABOUT THE BALANCE OF A MAN WITHOUT LEGS	/ 97
A DAMAGED THINKER #53	/ 99
A DAMAGED THINKER #56	/ 101
A DAMAGED THINKER #58	/ 103
TRANSFIXED IN MIDPAROXYSM	/ 105
RENAMING THE THINKER	/ 107
THERE IS SOME MATTER TOO SMALL TO BE FOUND BY THE LIGHT	/ 109
A DAMAGED THINKER #62	/ 111
A DAMAGED THINKER #63	/ 113
POEM #164 ABOUT THE THINKER BOMBING MAKES ME LAUGH	/ 115
A DAMAGED THINKER #72	/ 117
A DAMAGED THINKER #78	/ 119
A DAMAGED THINKER #83	/ 121
A DAMAGED THINKER #88	/ 123
LOOKING FOR INTIMACY IN THE NEVER WAS	/ 125
A LETTER TO AUGUSTE RODIN OFFERING TO HAVE HIM BE REBURIED IN CLEVELAND	/ 127
HE COULD BE A COUSIN	/ 129
A LETTER TO AUGUSTE RODIN FROM THE CUYAHOGA RIVER, CURRENTLY NOT ON FIRE	/ 131
A DAMAGED THINKER #93	/ 133
A DAMAGED THINKER #94	/ 135
A PILLOW FOR HIS HEAD	/ 137
A DIRECT CONTEMPLATION OF HELL	/ 139
FOR THE CHILD CONCEIVED IN CLEVELAND THE NIGHT THE THINKER WAS BOMBED	/ 141
I WANTED HIM TO LAUGH	/ 143
A CONSIPIRACY I LIKE	/ 145
IT'S MORE THAN JUST A WORK OF ART	/ 147
FOR NOW AND AFTER	/ 149
ANY NIGHT (PART OF THE WORLD)	/ 151

Bombing the Thinker Darren C. Demaree

A LETTER TO AUGUSTE RODIN ABOUT USELESS WINE

We've been mud

& bird

& dealt with

terrible loneliness

& we needed

a red that could

action us against

our own red,

but after you died

& he lost his legs,

the idea that we

needed

to be softened,

Bombing the Thinker Darren C. Demaree

become swamp

again was left

wanting

more bronze,

more marble.

1970

There were so many hearts

& so little clarity

in the 1960's that the acts

of those that kept their blood

high, running to drive

their point home with

a tremendous unlocking

of metal and stone, could

force revolution's river

straight through art's bend.

If it had been a painting,

they would have dragged

a razor's edge through it,

but since it was a man,

undeterred by bombs elsewhere

Bombing the Thinker Darren C. Demaree

they scrawled a message

on the base of the statue

& erased it, almost, with fire.

A UNIQUE AND HAUNTING BEAUTY

Melt the vernacular

of survival. Shape it

into a death mask

for the intentions

of the artist. If at some

point, the world pauses,

the thirst for more time

with beauty will

finally overwhelm us.

Until then, we don't

need to know what

would happen if

the bomb had been

as flawed as the reason.

Bombing the Thinker Darren C. Demaree

A DAMAGED THINKER #2

I was raised up to be
here. I was destroyed
to be here forever.

Bombing the Thinker Darren C. Demaree

A DAMAGED THINKER #3

Open body, taking

the lake wind

as my bride, could you

blame me for being lost

in such cold? I have

a heart that was never

proven real, but that

does not mean I deserved

to become your shrapnel.

Bombing the Thinker Darren C. Demaree

ALMOST THE POINT OF ART

With more than the tongue

out

& the elements surrounding

each foot in worship

of balance

& the removal of such balance,

I think dance

& painting do it best,

but that man in Cleveland,

classic, but contemporarily

flawed is almost perfect

in his destruction

of what we expect

Bombing the Thinker Darren C. Demaree

from the best of our art.

If he could stand up

& fall,

that panic would

seal the deal for me.

AN ACCEPTANCE OF ART

Show the whites

of your eyes

to be a lumbering

pair, not searching,

but searched for

& given, awarded

forever by the feather

of costume bird's

maker. I am willing

to be lied to. I am

desperate for it.

Bombing the Thinker Darren C. Demaree

BLOWN UP BY RADICAL PROTESTORS

How much salvation

could they dislodge

with their bomb placed

between The Thinker's

legs? This was dark

times they wanted filled

with light? He lost legs

& would have seen his

penis dart down the stairs

& across the street,

if his penis had been

Rodin's focus. It wasn't.

The Thinker's body

is slumped in thought

& if they had one real radical

Bombing the Thinker Darren C. Demaree

in their group they would

have taken that sad man's

head off, I mean, right?

IT WAS IMPERATIVE TO REMOVE THE OIL

Upkeep of the threatened,

they had to watch the oils

because they were trapping

too much dirt against

the second-coming

of the cradle of Cleveland's

Thinker. I like the gravitas

of an explosives victim willing

to be covered in oil. That

motherfucker was thick

with purpose. They removed

the oil because the visage

was dulled, not because he

was ever going to be safe

again. I like to think he found

an actual strength in facing

every fear, naked, a man

brash, kept whole by scars.

Bombing the Thinker Darren C. Demaree

A DAMAGED THINKER #12

Jump-cut the ecstatic

look my back provides

the birds. Sometimes,

if you are broad enough

of a man you must learn

to let shit roll down

your back. Mostly, I think

about fire rising to my face

but sometimes, without

any wind, all I can do

is think about the bird shit

& wonder about my hair.

Bombing the Thinker Darren C. Demaree

A DAMAGED THINKER #13

Tall stars, unable

to show my folded

belly any attention,

I would be a fool

to disdain the night

sky for returning

to me, despite

my sordid past

with the first morning

hour, but truly

I get angry at night

when there

is absolutely nothing

but the smoke

of old decisions

Bombing the Thinker Darren C. Demaree

& new threats

to my already crumbling

visage. I can tuck

almost a feather

in my ribs, that's how

close I am to flight.

A LETTER TO AUGUSTE RODIN, ASKING ABOUT HIS OTHER CASTS OF THE THINKER

Dark

& quiet,

would you

mind

terribly

if we

treated

your work

like crop

for our

politico

cowards?

Bombing the Thinker Darren C. Demaree

We need

more bronzed

& marbled men,

hulked

to their hull

& willing

to guard

the art.

NOT CROP, NOT HUSK

It must be terrible

to be all root

all the time,

like the sun

or the mother

of many children

& for big art

to be proven

to be the inside

of the apple,

it must be daunting

to know firmly

that you cannot be

eaten, that you

are the reason

Bombing the Thinker Darren C. Demaree

the energy finds

the energy

& all that rising.

AN EYE-CATCHING MEMORIAL OF MINDLESS VIOLENCE

Formation funeral,

we mourned

the old shape

of The Thinker,

because it placed

a black shell

deep in Cleveland,

gave fear to the still

people of Cleveland,

but once

the outrage finished

munching on

the tongue

of the vocal few,

I think we loved

Bombing the Thinker Darren C. Demaree

him more

for his survival

& how he took

that shot like we

imagine men can.

He was art

before, but now

he's special

to all of us.

A LETTER TO AUGUSTE RODIN, EXPLAINING THE BOMBING OF THE THINKER

The pedestal is just fine,

but your son, dear sir

has lost his legs

& yes, we've come up

with reasons why

somebody placed dynamite

like flowers at your grave.

We know there can be

no comfort for a dead man

about a cloned son

that never actually lived,

but this felt like the right

thing to do under such

circumstances. We've

Bombing the Thinker Darren C. Demaree

decided not to heal him.

He will remain un-alive.

He will be placed back on

his pedestal, without repair.

"DAMAGED 24TH OF MARCH 1970" WRITTEN IN SMALLER LETTERS

The inquiry

of the explosion,

the reversal-

attempt to force

the oddity

of the apocalyptic

into the beautiful

idea that though

we can think

of Hell as much

as we want,

there is no way

to imagine

a place into being.

Even that gift,

the temporary

firework of it

that opened

Bombing the Thinker Darren C. Demaree

nothing more

than a bizarre door

was, ultimately,

just a violent wall,

rejecting all

that try to pass

through it. We

learned then that

even if you whisper

the conclusion,

it doesn't actually

end anything.

THE RADICAL WEATHERMAN

Real fire finds whispering

to be a promise of more fire

& if these good people

with the right ideas about

the war, the wrong ideas

about what an enemy is,

wanted to leave a note

to make sure the art patrons

knew they had blown up

a superfluous bouquet

of the wealthy, then they

should have used less dynamite.

The explosion was the message

of war, but their reasons,

almost meaningless, pure

Bombing the Thinker Darren C. Demaree

misdirection, they mattered,

too? The statue they picked

was on the steps of the museum

& was free, open all the time

to every visitor, more than

a simple man performing

simply, really the kind of guy

they promised to be fighting for.

They just kept making mistakes.

A DAMAGED THINKER #16

Like every man who has seen fire
erupt from a metal casing, I believe
limits are the exotic animals

of this world. We know them
because we mourned their passing
slightly, before we swung, unloved

by the expired limitations, the color
of feather we can now only paint,
like we must create, again, a life

from the intended view of modern
memory, the fire that finds us,
our face, after it takes our legs

that was an animal, too, a live one.

Bombing the Thinker Darren C. Demaree

A DAMAGED THINKER #18

I am pedestal(ed),

that does not mean

I am inclined to be

a statue forever.

I got blown up once

forever. Confident

in the danger

of my own thoughts,

I am waiting, here

because the action

here, still comes to me

& I am fucking ready.

Bombing the Thinker Darren C. Demaree

A DAMAGED THINKER #20

Drive the moon

down, past knowledge

& beneath the cables

sewn up from the orchards

I've never seen, where

the artists make

their deals, where they

long to tease the diamond

tethers that dance

the firmament, gather

the beauty into the essence

of silence. I heard none

of the explosion, because I was

too taken by a neck that won't

move. I fell face-first. I felt

Bombing the Thinker Darren C. Demaree

cheated by the placement

of the dynamite. If I fell back,

I could have had the sky.

A DAMAGED THINKER #24

Muscle without bone,

my flesh-only fists

collects the spit-only

cruelty of time without

the punishment

of my assaulters. I want

them named, with Rodin,

as the men that made me

something to be seen.

Bombing the Thinker Darren C. Demaree

NO ONE WAS EVER ARRESTED

Most people

didn't care

that a statue

was blown up

& off the pedestal

& the reason why

mattered

even less. Cleveland

police searched

frantically for more

bombs, dynamite

grouped in threes

& since no wind

brought them ash,

the sulfur

smell that stayed

Bombing the Thinker Darren C. Demaree

hanging there

like a frustrating

cloud, unwilling

to simply rain

& get it over with,

they chased

everything, every-

where, until

the condensation

dissipated freely

& enough people

just forgot.

A LETTER TO AUGUSTE RODIN, ASKING ABOUT HIS OTHER CASTS OF THE THINKER

Dark

& quiet,

would you

mind

terribly

if we

treated

your work

like crop

for our

politico

cowards?

Bombing the Thinker Darren C. Demaree

We need

more bronzed

& marbled men,

hulked

to their hull

& willing

to guard

the art.

FREE FROM ARREST

They wanted art

to mean less

than human life

& they wanted

the money of art

to mean less

than human life

& they wanted

darkness to scare

those that loved art

into loving human

life more than art

& to be more cautious

with their money

when confronted

Bombing the Thinker Darren C. Demaree

with actual darkness.

They never understood

a single part of what

they were trying to do.

It was a rehearsal

of a doomed play.

The art, the money

& even the people

were always intertwined

& the war that made them

lose the feeling of all of that

took away the need

to punish their work.

A COLD AND LONELY PIECE OF ART

Lovely no more,

those thick ropes

of muscles appear

to have been braided

with a great anger

& the hunched look

is less pensive, now

that any rock forward

would autograph

the concrete. No crawl,

no smile, he's tucked

fear underneath

his bent wrists. He

stares at it intently,

afraid to raise up

Bombing the Thinker Darren C. Demaree

& join the scene,

afraid to move on,

forward, at any pace.

DEEP PITS

If there are whole worlds

missing, not shy, but taken

away by the physics

of revolution, then the only

new gleam found there

will be from other dynamite

lit to light the open dark

for a minute or so before

the wind, again, swallows

huge chunks of good spirit.

Bombing the Thinker Darren C. Demaree

FINISHING A SHERMAN LEE QUOTE

I hate to make

a definite promise

breathlessly,

I have only so many

words to explain

the unexplainable

& if you want to know

what I think about

bombs & art,

you will have to ask

me again, when

I can no longer

smell the ripping

of bronze. I would

cradle the man,

Bombing the Thinker Darren C. Demaree

as he would cradle

me, if you people

would allow such

time to elapse

before we decided

how to treat

a sculpture

that has gone to war

to never, ever return.

A DAMAGED THINKER #29

Hunched, I think

about the coffee

in every onlooker's

hand. I watch how

gentle they are with

heat. I care about

each of them. Do

you honestly think

I give a damn about

sugar in their drink?

Well, I do, I've missed

every useless thing.

Bombing the Thinker Darren C. Demaree

ORIGINALLY NAMED THE POET

The Thinker

was a soldier

last, but before

he even became

The Thinker

he was called

The Poet,

but when he

found Cleveland

he joined

the scene as

the big guy

Bombing the Thinker Darren C. Demaree

at the museum

& when he got

blown up, well,

he held on to

a bit of the fire

to be an Ohioan.

If he had stayed

simply The Poet

that fire would

have ruined him.

He stayed scarred.

He stayed here.

STABALIZED, WASHED, AND WAXED

The Thinker will never share

a tangerine with anyone else,

but in Cleveland there is an opening,

a dramatic scarring, an affair

that has made that thinker's struggle

human, a longing to be in a grove

again, untarnished, whole. Now

without legs & still considered art

& the memory of how no art is ever

finished being made into more art,

we tend to the upright, hunched man

like he is family, like he might

one day raise his head and crack

a smile for us. If he does, he will want

our fruit. We will give him everything.

Bombing the Thinker Darren C. Demaree

THE MONUMENT NOW REFLECTS THE ACTS OF INSANE MEN

This was Rodin's goal,
to show a man sinking
into torrid thought, bit
by the idea that he is
playing a game without
knowing all of the rules
& now, post-dynamite,
he still looks lost in salt-
water, oceans of almost
there now, but without
legs, the metal flowering
away from the pedestal,
it appears as if he might
finally be learning tides.

Bombing the Thinker Darren C. Demaree

A DAMAGED THINKER #34

I could level

my debts

with a nod.

Bombing the Thinker Darren C. Demaree

A DAMAGED THINKER #36

Lift the ten

political

hunters

to the helmet

of my blown

base, ask them

about thought

& thought

scattered.

Ask them why

I fear only

revolutions

without enough

gut to swallow

Bombing the Thinker Darren C. Demaree

me whole.

If I am to be

sacrificed again

I don't want

a single piece

of my bronze

choked upon.

A DAMAGED THINKER #38

I have learned all of the silent things.

I have learned all of the roaring.

There is nothing I can say to people.

Bombing the Thinker Darren C. Demaree

A DAMAGED THINKER #40

I would leave a note

for the director, I

would simply leave

& abandon my use

as a landscape

for the Ohio academics,

I would go back

to Europe, for a while,

maybe find a Greek

with both of her arms

gone, lost to time

& looters, we could

try not to lose too much

skin as we rested against

Bombing the Thinker Darren C. Demaree

each other. I would

never actually leave

a note. I would leave

& owe them nothing

more than my absence.

"THE LAST OPTION OF MOUNTING THE SCULPTURE IN ITS DAMAGED STATE ALSO HAD SIGNIFICANT ETHICAL IMPLICATIONS"

–Bruce Christman

Months of questions, dipping
toes into the flavorless pudding
of questions that the artist
was too dead to answer
& yet there were options
& interpretations of Rodin's practice
that could have nothing to do
with what he might do if someone
decided to stick dynamite
between the legs of his fleshy,
metal son. They shoved him
back to the front, like this was
a war he was need for. He wasn't
needed, he'd taken the hit well,

Bombing the Thinker Darren C. Demaree

but once you have the pedestal

in place it's tough to give up

the statue. We still love

the artist's best, even if loss

has been sewn into the muchness.

Let's say the steps carried that

twenty-minute fear forever,

but the new, living feet that crossed

the missing legs of that cast

of The Thinker, had to feel

doubly blessed by the decision.

THERE WAS STILL A PEDESTAL

Nuclei of the determined

spirits of Cleveland, I'm not

really sure you needed a man

without working shoulders,

but you had his dedication

& when he was felled by desire

without thought, there was

still a pedestal that waited

for Cleveland to promise

to fill. For a while, they embraced

the momentum, they beat

the scenario with an open space,

a lazy frame for a city that never

needed to own art, but did

Bombing the Thinker Darren C. Demaree

because art is always pulling

close to other art, creating a home
undefeatable by simple dynamite.
You may not know this,

but Cleveland has always been whole.
What appears to be missing, there,
is only rust-belt brilliance, paused.

WHERE THE HEAD AND SHOULDER HIT THE PAVEMENT

You don't have to make poetry

out of the dead parts of Ohio,

but when something so beautiful-

ly slow is launched to die, angled

against the coldest cement, almost

a corpse, but without a full crumple,

there is a running to rally around

his planting location. He could

never grow there, but the shadows

that reached down from the museum

would have new roots tangling

& reaching to wave, moving with

the sun, but akin to something in

line with the best of winds. We

righted his figure, but we did not

do it because he needed us to.

Bombing the Thinker Darren C. Demaree

INCRALAC COATING

I have un-basic questions

about the limp

& feel sorry for

of an air-drying coat

that never gets credit

for holding the art in

& never gets to hold alone

anything. A solvent

nature can be a curse.

Bombing the Thinker Darren C. Demaree

A DAMAGED THINKER #47

Torn flame,

I am dancing

without

movement

& without

brethren

to do more

than lap heat,

as if something

bronzed could

have a tongue

or real moves

at all. I'm not

really needed,

Bombing the Thinker Darren C. Demaree

but I feel

integral

to the hot tide

of the past.

A DAMAGED THINKER #48

Sight kettles

my time

as vibrancy.

Think again

about

no choices

I have made.

Sight has

stewed me

& the physics

of a cooked

world,

has done

very little

Bombing the Thinker Darren C. Demaree

to take

this taste

out my tight-

lipped mouth.

ALMOST FREE

The quick tuck

of the explosion,

must have looked

like a bird's wing

preparing to

unleash defiance

to bound nature

& that second before

the fire shoved

him backwards

with both hands,

must have felt

like he was almost

alive, like he was

Bombing the Thinker Darren C. Demaree

more than Rodin.

CHASING THE LOGIC OF A BOMBING

The sound

wants to stay,

but the force

pales the metal

& flees

the desert

of no stars

& that world

cannot be still

long enough

to matter

without

Bombing the Thinker Darren C. Demaree

claiming

the ecstatic

of the art.

When the echo

gropes the echo

& the pressure

fades into

itself, all

that never

mattered

eats forever

in blankness.

AN AVOIDANCE OF ART

      after Danielle Pafunda

You're going

to ditch

all these bodies?

Bombing the Thinker Darren C. Demaree

A LETTER TO AUGUSTE RODIN ABOUT THE BALANCE OF A MAN WITHOUT LEGS

That possibility

of dancing again

is gone. Even

if he never danced

before it must be

a great loss of spirit

to become only

the thing that you

were intended to be.

Bombing the Thinker Darren C. Demaree

A DAMAGED THINKER #53

Almost mute,

I speak when

the wind speaks

& with that

rough language,

I have salt

on my tongue

from Lake Erie

& the ships

that caught fire

& sank, they

sing to me

in a language,

too, one of envy

Bombing the Thinker Darren C. Demaree

for my metal's

willingness

to be blown

& remain blown

& above

the water's cool,

lapping burial.

A DAMAGED THINKER #56

If Rodin knew

what explosives

could do to metal,

would I have

a whole ocean

rising behind me

or actual flames

from Hell, licking

the nape of my neck?

If Rodin knew

this could happen

he would have

done it himself

& done it again

Bombing the Thinker Darren C. Demaree

& again, successfully.

A DAMAGED THINKER #58

Forest of open people,

I am your un-human

king. Toss your foreign

offering at where my feet

used to be. This will mean

much more to you.

Bombing the Thinker Darren C. Demaree

TRANSFIXED IN MIDPAROXYSM

I just thought

that his body

looked more active

after the bombing

& apparently

I was right,

I was right

& apparently

that was cruelty.

Bombing the Thinker Darren C. Demaree

RENAMING THE THINKER

Warped slope

of a French

lightning

bug's mind,

I want to claim

you as our own,

give you new

purpose, a little

agility to a life

permanently

perched, torn up

& mattering

so much more

as a survivor

of such confused

Bombing the Thinker Darren C. Demaree

men. Let's call

you Nick. That

flash to take

your folding

& tucked

& tore it off,

that happened

to the other,

simple guy.

THERE IS SOME MATTER TOO SMALL TO BE FOUND BY THE LIGHT

Actual science

& actual art,

those black dots

that are never named

can never be framed

or sold as formula

& that ornery wrinkle

of process

& flailing, even in

victory

keeps us cold

enough to know

Bombing the Thinker Darren C. Demaree

that the light

itself is black dots,

ecstatic dancers

bouncing off each

other, creating

believable energy.

A DAMAGED THINKER #62

For my part, I sat there

knowing one day my angry

peace would take a shot

from compromised Ohio,

always taking a beaten,

never actually beaten Ohio

& there I would be, strong,

wide enough to survive

the explosions, like Ohio.

I resumed my post without

a single arrest of Ohio

& we just went on

from there, with our fear

packed into our wounds, so

Bombing the Thinker Darren C. Demaree

it could be worth something.

A DAMAGED THINKER #63

I am a cave

for myself.

I am open

to be a cave

for you.

I thought

I was

a mountain,

I was

very wrong

& I was

very wrong.

Bombing the Thinker Darren C. Demaree

POEM #164 ABOUT THE THINKER BOMBING MAKES ME LAUGH

Shoulder deep

in the bombing,

what it means

about art

& cowards,

what it means

to survive,

damaged

& un-repaired,

what the police

didn't do,

what the director

struggled with

Bombing the Thinker Darren C. Demaree

& today

I am hysterical

with the thought

that maybe he

just tried

to stand up

after a hundred years

of weight

& thought

he fell, splayed

against the concrete,

his legs bronzed

& asleep from effort,

his embarrassment

too much to explain.

A DAMAGED THINKER #72

after James Wright

If there was ever a river

that snaked near enough

to my stiff-footed actions,

it always died, dried up

before it ever splashed

my pedestal. Thrown,

I tried to swim in concrete,

because there was only

the promise of water,

the beauty of water

& with the ground shaking

terribly beneath us, it lost

Bombing the Thinker Darren C. Demaree

the momentum to find me.

A river is always a river,

even when it's gone

or on fire, so, once I had

been forced to dive, I swam

forever on those steps.

A DAMAGED THINKER #78

I would expect a crowd

in good wind, to see

if the residual energy

of Ohio has collected enough

perk to set me free, to sign

me up for the National Guard?

I'd take a weapon. I'd use it

in a war or near a war. I just

want watch the little bugger

eat through a quiet person.

I don't want them to die.

I want them stay partial.

Bombing the Thinker Darren C. Demaree

A DAMAGED THINKER #83

You wouldn't think

much about crippling

a pearl. I do. I do.

Bombing the Thinker Darren C. Demaree

A DAMAGED THINKER #88

Every flame

is a lover

you wished

would stop

kissing you

& just get it

over with.

Coy fire,

next bomb,

there's more

of me to

consume.

Bombing the Thinker Darren C. Demaree

LOOKING FOR INTIMACY IN THE NEVER WAS

I have a problem
alone. I quit
drinking so I am

alone all the time
now. Every time
I visit the museum

I leave him a note.
He doesn't drink
either. He doesn't

write back either,
but I'm used to that.
When I return,

the old letter is gone
& there is an opening

Bombing the Thinker Darren C. Demaree

for a new letter.

That was all I ever
needed, to not pile
up in a public place.

I imagine the museum
is collecting my letters
in a file somewhere.

Some day all of these
fragments will make us
both feel quite whole.

A LETTER TO AUGUSTE RODIN OFFERING TO HAVE HIM BE REBURIED IN CLEVELAND

Forget the catalog, there must
have been some actual DNA
in those boys, even if by accident,

you could not cast twenty of them
& not nick your own flesh
& even if now you have no flesh

to call your own anymore,
there is still a wounded family
for you to return to. That part

of time is where actual grace
resides. There will be no angels,
but there can be a reunion of sorts.

Bombing the Thinker Darren C. Demaree

HE COULD BE A COUSIN

I have cousins, large men

that move differently than I do

& when the cool sea air

finds them they handle it

well. I am giddy near salt.

That folded, hulking man

in Cleveland, he could be

a cousin of mine as well,

or I could just tell stories

about him that make it seem

like we are related in some way.

He's French, but he's been

in Ohio, all the way through

many generations of Ohio,

Bombing the Thinker Darren C. Demaree

felt the full weight of Ohio

& when I place my hands
where his feet used to be,
he grants me such liberties

& when I contemplate
the awfulness of contemplation
only, I feel something for him.

A LETTER TO AUGUSTE RODIN FROM THE CUYAHOGA RIVER, CURRENTLY NOT ON FIRE

There are moments

for dragons,

where it looks like

dragons have visited

Northern Ohio

& most of the time

that is only drug-

related talk,

but I talked to your Thinker

at a meeting,

a victim's alliance thing

& I think, maybe,

Bombing the Thinker Darren C. Demaree

you should know

that he is sure,

utterly convinced,

that dragons are real.

A DAMAGED THINKER #93

Holes

aren't

light.

Bombing the Thinker Darren C. Demaree

A DAMAGED THINKER #94

Steps, hard banks

of my artscape,

each one good

to bully the burial,

each one shoving

me back up

on that goddamn

pedestal, prison

of the work

of a heaven

so fallible that

explosives found it.

Bombing the Thinker Darren C. Demaree

A PILLOW FOR HIS HEAD

I can no longer unravel

my own wish to finish

off The Thinker. My first

desire, once I saw the old

photos was to comfort

him, take away the harsh

angle of his head on the steps

& grant him a certain time

where there were none,

no expectations of his pose

& no mourning of his current

state. Now, I think that if

I had the chance I might

smother him completely

Bombing the Thinker Darren C. Demaree

with a forever kind of comfort

& if he struggles, if he really

believes he needs more time

to evaluate existence

& judge the tethers of this plane

& heaven, of this plane

& hell, I can answer that

for him, with my own weight.

He would be so peaceful

if he was only a statue.

A DIRECT CONTEMPLATION OF HELL

Face down, brilliance

of brilliance,

cast to never decide

more than the confirmation

that we are the tether,

the unregenerate collection

of muscle, given to flight,

but never giving the room

to fly. Removing the base,

they dared to change

the world with explosives,

which is a common dare,

but they put that statue

face-flush to the window

of the rootless area,

the concrete steps

of the art museum, hell

to anyone or anything

Bombing the Thinker Darren C. Demaree

that loves real beauty.

FOR THE CHILD CONCEIVED IN CLEVELAND THE NIGHT THE THINKER WAS BOMBED

Thin layer of separation

between the boom

& that boom, with-

holding the whole volume

of energy that was created

by both acts, did you feel

the pool shake when

you swam home to home?

If you were in a movie,

this might make you

an incredible character.

If you knew what happened

so close to your first dive

into the ecstatic, I'd think

you'd carry that like a badge

& wield power you never,

ever earned a piece of.

Bombing the Thinker Darren C. Demaree

I WANTED HIM TO LAUGH

I brought the ladder

quickly from the car

& before security

could video me

& make it down

the front steps

of the Cleveland

Museum of Art,

I had made it all

the way to his ear

& had started in

on the dirtiest joke

I could think of

& before they tore

Bombing the Thinker Darren C. Demaree

the ladder

out from under me
& wrestled me down,
all four of them.

I completed the joke
& the fine I paid
seemed worth it,

to give him the profane
& sincere gift
of absolute distraction.

A CONSIPIRACY I LIKE

The moon

bombed

Cleveland's

Thinker

for revenge,

for Neil Armstrong,

an Ohioan,

dragging his heels

across her face

a year before.

It was love

& rough love

gone really wrong.

The Thinker

never spoke

Bombing the Thinker Darren C. Demaree

to Neil again.

The moon

never spoke

to Neil again,

or so we're told.

IT'S MORE THAN JUST A WORK OF ART

Hip bone

to hip bone,

the bunting

of a crowd

pressed

together

can make

a city

more like

a tide

overwhelming

all of time

& if that

broken man

weighed less

Bombing the Thinker Darren C. Demaree

he would

weigh less
for all of us
& we could
carry him

like we always
promise
veterans
we will carry

them, then
he could captain
the ships
we have raised

to be frozen
above Ohio.

FOR NOW AND AFTER

I took my children

to see The Thinker

in Cleveland

& when I lifted them

up to touch the escaping

bronze from just above

the pedestal, like that

is what has driven away

his legs in a slow tide

of re-evaluation

& when each of them

touched what remained

of his calf, they did so

gingerly, knowing

Bombing the Thinker Darren C. Demaree

& not knowing

that what we were doing

was against the rules

& that feeling

was what I wanted to give

them. The oldest child,

the girl, is convinced

that he looked at her

& that he didn't like

how tender she was.

ANY NIGHT (PART OF THE WORLD)

We create

multiple salvations

with every piece

of humanity

we re-create

& it is only

our forgetfulness

that leads

to the wobbling

of our other work.

Stare at the first

promise.

It has nothing

Bombing the Thinker Darren C. Demaree

to do with God.

It is fullness

& the time for more.

www.ingramcontent.com/pod-product-compliance
Lightning Source LLC
Chambersburg PA
CBHW030439010526
44118CB00011B/717